ALICE IN WORMLAND:
SELECTED POEMS

Alice in Wormland
SELECTED POEMS
DOROTHY HEWETT
EDITED BY EDNA LONGLEY

BLOODAXE BOOKS

Copyright © Dorothy Hewett 1968, 1975, 1979, 1987, 1990
Foreword © Edna Longley 1990

ISBN: 1 85224 125 X

First published 1990 by
Bloodaxe Books Ltd,
P.O. Box 1SN,
Newcastle upon Tyne NE99 1SN.

Bloodaxe Books Ltd acknowledges
the financial assistance of Northern Arts.

Typesetting by Bryan Williamson, Darwen, Lancashire.

Printed in Great Britain by
Billing & Sons Limited, Worcester.

For my daughter Kate

Acknowledgements

This book includes poems from the following collections by Dorothy Hewett, all published in Australia: *Windmill Country* (Overland, 1968), *Rapunzel in Suburbia* (Prism, 1975), *Greenhouse* (Big Smoke Books, 1979) and *Alice in Wormland* (Paper Bark Press, 1987). The selection was made by Edna Longley for Bloodaxe Books, in consultation with Dorothy Hewett.

Contents

Foreword

'I am Eve, spitting the pips in the eye of the myth-makers...' declares the narrator of 'Legend of the Green Country'. She might be voicing the spirit of Dorothy Hewett's poetic achievement. With her energy of imagination and rhythm, her power to unmake myths and to make her own, Hewett is a major figure in the history of Australian poetry. She is also a major figure in the history of women's poetry, into which she has introduced a new persona – the 'adventurous woman'. Hewett's 'Beata Beatrix' reflects, as she begins to write her own story:

> *in life one must accept the limitations*
> *no one has ever loved an adventurous woman*

When Hewett the adventurous woman poet 'speaks her truth', she challenges and disturbs both sexes.

Dorothy Hewett's adventure moves from the salt-threatened greenery of Western Australia to a fascination with Sydney's 'beauty, squalor and turbulence'. In the preface to her only novel *Bobbin Up* (1959; reprinted 1985 by Virago) she tells how she left Perth and her first husband to live, with her boiler-maker lover, among the Sydney working class as a Communist activist. *Bobbin Up* is based on a year she spent working and proselytising in a grim woollen mill. Hewett's anarchistic talent was largely silenced by her deference to Marxist orthodoxy, whose prescriptions included social realism. She did, however, break the silence with *Bobbin Up*, where her acute eye and ear humanise social realism, even if the injections of Party dogma (as she now acknowledges) don't work. In 1968, in her mid-forties, Hewett renounced an ideology 'which had organised my life for something like twenty-three years', 'got back my identity', and found that she could write again. (See Candida Baker's interview with Hewett in *Yacker*; Picador, 1986.) She has since published six books of poems and become a successful and controversial playwright.

In *Bobbin Up* the collective lives of women mill-workers take on an epic quality. The novel's poetic and rural counterpart is 'Legend of the Green Country': mythic as well as epic, a mother-narrative of Australia, and surely a great poem. Hewett invokes the green country as the place of both colonial and creative origin:

> this was my country, here I go back for nurture
> To the dry soaks, to the creeks running salt through the timber,
> To the ghosts of the sandalwood cutters, and the blue breath of their fires,
> To the navvies in dark blue singlets laying rails in the scrub.

Yet the poem's life-affirming 'rip and run' meets cross-currents of greed and guilt. Hewett's legend is also a lament: for 'the land falling into the cash register'; for farms depopulated and made barren by a ruthless economic system; for primal innocence; for paradise not only lost but despoiled. On several levels 'Legend of the Green Country' seems a legend of the green earth itself.

Throughout Hewett's poetry, ruined Eden is a sexual as well as a colonial motif. Her versions of Adam and Eve do not necessarily spare Eve. In 'Legend of the Green Country' women are mostly aligned with the salt, the sour, the miserly, the frigid: 'The women were strong and they destroyed the men, / Lying locked and cold in their sexless beds.' Perhaps, as in Patrick Kavanagh's *The Great Hunger*, the poem shows men and women differently trapped by a nexus of economic necessity and puritanical *mores*. For Hewett, this epitomises bourgeois society in general.

But if the great sin of coldness, of emotional parsimony, can be committed by either sex, Hewett portrays father-figures more positively than mother-figures: 'From mother to daughter the curse drops like a stone'. Greeting menstruation as indeed a curse, the mother in Hewett's poetry appears to repress her daughter's creativity along with her sexuality. The mother's metaphorical death, as for some other women writers, may be a condition of the artist's birth. Hewett has said of her poems:

> I'm not in my life a particularly violent person, but there must be a great residue of violence and obsession and – what else – maybe guilt, and maybe anger, hidden away there which comes out in the poetry. Poetry taps all these hidden things in oneself more than any other form of writing. [*Yacker*, p.178]

Whether reacting against matriarchal, patriarchal or communist straitjackets, Hewett's poetry seeks to liberate the *id*. She simultaneously liberates fairy-tale and fantasy as the means to tap 'hidden things', as the medium of psychic adventure. Thus in 'Grave Fairy Tale', her brilliant rewriting of Rapunzel, the witch's 'posturing blackness, savage as a cuckoo' enacts the destructiveness of repression and denial. The adventures of Alice with Nim, 'sinister boy' and male Muse, are Hewett's most elaborate attempt to work through and redeem what has gone wrong in the garden. But, as when 'Miss Hewett's Shenanigans' ironises 'Some day my prince will come', the poems also expose the dark side of sexuality itself and do not guarantee happy endings.

Dorothy Hewett's poetry unusually combines dramatic narrative with lyricism, an extroverted manner with an introverted content. She now lives in Sydney 'on a major road with a brothel next door'. This extreme location suggests how compulsively her imagination is attracted to 'the sense of some sort of energy and life going on in the world'. Hewett's poems, too, are situated at the pulse of life. They transmit to the reader an extraordinary electric charge.

EDNA LONGLEY

FROM **WINDMILL COUNTRY**
(1968)

Legend of the Green Country

I

September is the spring month bringing tides, swilling green in the
    harbour mouth,
Turnabout dolphins rolling-backed in the rip and run, the king
    waves
Swinging the coast, snatching at fishermen from Leeuwin to Norah's
    Head;
A dangerous month: but I count on an abacus as befits a shopkeeper's
    daughter.
I never could keep count by modern methods, the ring of the till
Is profit and loss, the ledger, hasped with gold, sits in its heavy dust
On the counter, out front the shopkeeper's sign hangs loose and
    bangs in the wind,
The name is obliterated, the dog swells and stinks in the gutter,
The golden smell of the beer does not run in the one street, like
    water,
The windmill head hangs, broken-necked, flapping like a great plain
    turkey
As the wind rises … this was my country, here I go back for nurture
To the dry soaks, to the creeks running salt through the timber,
To the ghosts of the sandalwood cutters, and the blue breath of their
    fires,
To the navvies in dark blue singlets laying rails in the scrub.

My grandfather rode out, sawing at a hard-mouthed ginger horse,
And a hard heart in him, a dray full of rum and beer, bully-beef and
    treacle,
Flour and tea, workboots and wideawakes with the corks bobbing
    for flies;
Counting the campfires in the dusk, counting the men, counting the
    money,
Counting the sheep from the goats, and the rack-rented railway
    houses.
No wonder I cannot count for the sound of the money-changers,
The sweat and the clink, the land falling into the cash register,
Raped and eroded, thin and black as a myall girl on a railway siding.

He came back, roaring and singing up from the gullies, his beard
Smelt of rum, his money-bag plump as a wild duck under his saddle.
The old horse stumbled in the creek-bed but brought him home,
The dray rattled; as they took him down in the yard he cursed and
    swore
At the dream, and blubbered for it: next Saturday night he rode his
    horse
Up the turkey red carpet into the bar, smashing the bottles and
    glasses,
Tipping the counter, sending the barmaid screaming, her breasts
    tilting with joy.
The great horse reared and he sang and swore and flung his hat at
    the sky,
And won his bets, and rode home, satisfied, to a nagging wife and
    daughter,
Having buried his pain and his lust under the broken bottles.
The publican swept them up in the cold light next morning,
And that was the end of it, they thought, but it wasn't so easy:
There is no end to it and I stand at the mole watching the sea run out,
Or hang over the rails at the Horseshoe Bridge and listen to the tide,
Listen to the earth that pleasured my grandfather with his flocks
    and acres
Drowned under salt, his orange-trees forked bare as unbreeched
    boys.
Only the apples, little and hard, bitten green and bitter as salt,
They come up in the spring, in the dead orchard they are the fruit
Of our knowledge, and I am Eve, spitting the pips in the eye of the
    myth-makers.
This is my legend; an old man on a ginger horse who filled his till
And died content with a desert, or so they said: his stone angel
Cost a pretty penny, but the workmanship was faulty, its wings curve
In a great arc over the graveyard, it grows mildewed and dirty,
Its nose is syphilitic, its feet splay like a peasant, its hands
Clasp over its breast like the barmaid who screamed in the pub,
And kissed him, for love, not money, but only once.

II

My grandmother had a bite like a sour green apple,
Little and pitiless she kept the till,
Counted the profits, and stacked the bills of sale.
She bought the shops and the farms, the deeds were hers,
In the locked iron safe with a shower of golden sovereigns.
She never trusted the banks, they failed in the nineties,
She kept her bank notes rolled in the top of her stocking,
Caressingly, while her prices soared and dropped,
Her barometer; crops and wool and railway lines.
Each night she read the news by the hurricane lantern,
While the only child wept for love in the washing-up water.
She could argue like a man, politics, finance, banking.
In her rocking chair with her little dangling feet,
Her eyes glittered like broken beer bottle glass.
She kept one eye out for a farmer to spend his money
And a sharp tongue for a borrowing mate of my grandfather's.

Once, long ago, in Swanston Street she "made"
For fashionable ladies, their breasts half bared
And their ankles covered, pads in their hair,
Bustles, bugle beads and jet, dyed ostrich feathers,
You could see their shadows waving from hansom cabs,
And the ghostly wheels turning into Swanston Street.
She had her miracles and quoted them...
Science and Health by Mary Baker Eddy,
She read *The Monitor* while the dust storms whirled,
And marvelled that God was love; it was all clear profit.
She wet the bagging to filter the westerlies,
Planted geraniums and snowdrops under the tank,
And squashed black caterpillars on moonlit forays.
She balanced the ledger and murmured, 'God is love,'
Feeling like God, she foreclosed on another farm.

She never read for pleasure, or danced or sang,
Or listened with love, slowly life smote her dumb,
Till she lay in the best bedroom, pleating the quilt,
In a fantasy of ball dresses for Melbourne ladies.
Her eyes were remote as pennies, her sheets stank,
She cackled and counted a mythical till all her days.

III

My father was a black-browed man who rode like an Abo.
The neighbours gossiped, 'A touch of the tarbrush there.'
He built the farm with his sweat, it lay in the elbow
Of two creeks, thick with wattle and white ti-tree.
At night he blew on the cornet; once, long ago, he'd played
On the pleasure cruises that went up the Yarra on Saturday nights;
The lights bobbed in the muddy water, the girls in white muslin sang
    Tipperary.
Now he played in the lonely sleepout, looking out over the flat,
With the smell of creekwater, and a curlew crying like a murdered
    gin,
Crying all night, till he went out with a shotgun and finished its
    screaming,
But not his own...he, the mendicant, who married the storekeeper's
    daughter.

My mother was a dark round girl in a country town,
With down on her lip, her white cambric blouse
Smelt of roses and starch, she was beautiful,
Warm, and frigid in a world of dried-up women,
Aborting themselves with knitting needles on farms.
She wept in the tin humpy at the back of the store,
For the mother who hated, the father who drank
And loved her; then, sadly, she fell in love
And kissed the young accountant who kept the books,
Behind the ledgers, the summer dust on the counters.
He was on the booze, broke all his promises,
Went off to the city and sang in an old spring cart,
'Bottle-oh, Bottle-oh' till his liver gave out
And he died; she married in arum lilies, satin, tulle,
Under the bell that tolled for the storekeeper's daughter.
Men shot themselves in the scrub on her wedding day.
My father brought her wildflowers, rode forty miles,
But he never kissed like the beautiful bottle-oh,
Boozing in the pub like a fly caught in its amber.

The roof of the hospital cracked like purgatory,
At sunset the birth blood dried on the sheets,
Nobody came to change them, the sun went down,
The pain fell on her body like a beast and mauled it.

She hated the farm, hated the line of wattles
Smudging the creek, kept her hands full of scones,
Boiled the copper, washing out sins in creek water,
Kept sex at bay like the black snake coiled in the garden,
Burning under the African daisies and bridal creeper,
Took her children to bed, he lay alone in the sleep-out,
With a headache and *The Seven Pillars of Wisdom*.
The girls in their picture hats came giggling and singing,
Trailing their hands like willows from the Yarra launches,
Till the dream was nightmare and all his life a regret,
Bought and gelded in an old grey house by a creek-bed.

IV

My grandfather rode round the sheep in leggings, and fed the calves,
He mended the gates, once a month he drove into town to his
        "lodge",
A white carnation picked at dusk from my grandmother's garden,
A dress suit with a gold watch, a chain looped over his belly,
Magnificent!...but my father only grinned sourly and read
        Remarque's
All Quiet on the Western Front, while my mother polished his medals
For Anzac Day. They never understood him, none of the shopkeepers'
        breed,
Christ! how could they? They only had a copy of the Bible,
My grandmother quoted it (mostly wrong), and Tennyson bound
        in morocco,
The Stag at Bay on the sitting-room wall, two elephants from Bombay,
Spoil from the trip they took "home"...was it a century ago?
The piano where, once a year, we sang hymns, when the minister
        came.
They had no religion, they believed in themselves, no other,
Self-made men and women who sat round their groaning table,
While all the no-hopers were taken over by the banks,
Or walked off, and took up dead-end jobs in the city;
The farms lay at their boundaries breeding dust and rabbits.
They breasted it all, the waves of drought and depression,
Of flood and fire, sown in sparks from the black steam trains
Roaring through wheat and the dead white grass by the sidings.
Their haystacks burnt as gold as their money bags, their till
Was full of horses drooling on oats and rock salt, of cows

With udders streaming white milk in the frosty mornings,
Of roosters crowing their triumph from the stable roof, and orchards,
Green as their hopes, tangy with peach, cradled with quail and
     oranges.
Only the sheep bleating their thin cry on the winter evenings,
Echoed the crows, the scavengers that were our kinsmen.
The woolly ghosts cropped the grass to its roots; the hard hoofs
Beat a track to the end of a world where the creeks ran dry,
The lambs lay blind while the crows ate their eyes in the salmon
     gums,
And the timberless paddocks blew in dust as far as the sea.

V

Only the man with the cornet, who rode with Remarque
Across his saddle bows, only he loved the soil,
Running it through his fingers he sensed its dying,
Its blowing away on the winds of time and cut timber,
He saw the salt of its death rising.
He said, 'I have a plan', and rode with it into the cities,
A plan for trees, acres of trees blowing by creekbeds,
Forests marching in long green lines to save a country,
Picking up their roots and digging them into the earth,
Holding it fast against the salt and the wind tides.
But the laughter rose in gales from the men in cities,
Their desks shook, their papers scattered like almond blossom in
     storm,
'Visionary'…'Dreamer…go back to the bend in two creeks,
Thick with wattle and ti-tree you have grown to love,
Go back and wait for the trees to wither, the creek to run,
Drowned in salt, for this is your heritage…'
'Years from now we will not be sitting here, we will be gone',
And where will you go, man the great Dreamer…dead and the land
     dead,
Only your ghost will ride like an Abo, crying *Trees* through the
     corrugated iron
Of the sidings, where the rails buckle with heat and men sit smoking
And brooding on a green world, as you once dreamed of Gippsland,
Under the fern-choked water, falling, falling: you tried to give us
A vision of greenness and water, who were bred out of desert and
     scrub
And sheep crying and crow…our father whispered *Trees* as he blew
     Tipperary.

VI

The women were strong and they destroyed the men,
Lying locked and cold in their sexless beds,
Putting greed in their men's fingers instead of love.
They drove them from the earth, left them derelict,
Dead mutton hanging on hooks on the verandahs.
For them the curlew wailed, the old horse lay
Trapped in the paddock all night with rheumaticky haunches.
My grandfather wept, 'Whoa back there Ginger, whoa back,'
Till the glasses winked in the bar like barmaids' eyes,
The virgins in muslin, the pretty French girls from Marseilles,
And a little whore in the rain on Princess Bridge.
Where would they go, rich, gelded and blind,
Tugging their old mad women with them to their graves?

VII

This land is not mine to give or trade,
I have no lien on these sad acres,
Where the crow flies home,
A solitary reaper.
The milky creek runs death,
The wattle and the ti-tree are all gone.
My father went, exiled himself in cities,
Sour as a green apple, his tap-root broken.

The orchard lies a nameless graveyard
Behind the farm, stripped of its flowers and fruit,
Its trees, its birds, its bees murmuring.
Only the skull of a sheep dropped at the cross-roads,
And the rattling dray in the scrub on the empty skyline,
My grandfather yelling, 'Whoa back there Ginger, whoa back,
While I carry my money bags home through the heart of this country.'
The wheels of the old dray turning, bring us full circle,
Death whirls in the wind, the old house hunches in on itself
And sleeps like the blind, *The Stag at Bay* hangs skewed
On the wall, the elephants from Bombay are chipped by the children,
Nobody plays *Rock of Ages* on the untuned piano now.
But the crows cry over my salty acres, scavengers come home
To roost and foul their nests in the creaking gum trees.

VIII

Who rises from the dead each spring must pay the cost.
How shall I pay living at the harbour's mouth
Where my father's ghost sits mumbling over breakfast,
Nodding at headlines, full of strikes and wool boards,
Tariffs to sink his teeth into, wars for his grandsons,
Where's Remarque now! His medals on the wall blink
Their derision, his heart's grown crooked, out of season.
He forgets how to sink a well or plant a tree.
His back's like sandlewood, his smell is sweet with death.
He crumbles where he sits, the tide rises to his lips.
Mother to daughter the curse drops like a stone.
My mother sits silent with nothing to remember.

Yet sometimes in the dark I come upon him in his chair,
A book lying open on his knees, his eye turned inward,
And then he sings old songs of Bendigo and windlasses,
And tells me tales of Newport railway workers, Nellie Melba
Singing High Mass, and how he read all night in Collingwood,
Voted for Labor and fell in love with Nellie Stewart.
But never a word of that far green country of his spirit,
Where the trees grow greener than the Gippsland grass.
All this is locked away in grief and salt.
Maybe, in death, his lips will whisper it,
And the green vision that gave sap to all his days
Will rise again and give him back his country.

IX

This is *my* truth, a grandfather boozed with guilt
And gold, who got free kisses from a barmaid for his gift,
And a great horse that swung its rump and tilted the world down.
A man rides through the windmill country like an Abo,
Blowing his cornet in a wail of *Trees*, bewitched
By Gippsland fern and luminous girls mirrored in the Yarra.
I will pay this debt, go back and find my place,
Pick windfalls out of the grass like a mendicant.
The little sour apples still grow in my heart's orchard,
Bitten with grief, coming up out of the dead country.
Here I will eat their salt and speak my truth.

The Burial

He couldn't have expected to die on holiday,
Beneath that mountain, within close call of the sea.
Yet he came here every year, he must have known
It would have to be here or there, asleep or awake,
Between the fall of a sparrow or flight of a bee.

After the platitudes in the Methodist pews,
Abide with Me and the vulgar veneered coffin,
(We asked for jarrah), and the blustery wind outside
Blowing the ladies' church hats into the harbour,
It was a relief to stand at the clayey grave
And listen to the parson clanging his dust and ashes.
You can't do much to pretty up that ceremony.

'He was a man who achieved much honour,' the parson said,
'A man who reaped his reward and died content.'
How bitter the grin wreathing those iron jaws,
Locked in the paltry coffin with the hymns in his ears.
Come home to his own, my father, rich in nothing
But the money that lay like pennies over his eyes.

His mother, that immigrant woman, once sang, long ago,
In her rich contralto in this same grey church on the harbour,
Till the parson asked her to stay and join the choir.
Well, *he's* staying here now, but I was the only singer,
His atheist daughter to whom he had nothing to leave.

We buried him in the dark scrub, the gulls flashed out at sea.
An old man teetered at the hole, read Rupert Brooke
And 'They shall not grow old': this was the final irony.
They were all so old, telling tales about French girls and gyppos,
It was hard to imagine any of them had been young.
Yet that ragged boy chasing cows in the Gippsland fern,
Scaring the crows off the clover, had died a rich man.

He was honoured with medals, sprinkled with red cloth poppies,
The king of the Belgians had kissed him on both his cheeks,
But couldn't warm them; there was some canker he carried
Into the earth with him, I don't think he'll grow good flowers

Or sleep in peace, he had insomnia badly these last few years,
It was that Methodist conscience giving him hell.

Remember him, leaping off the troop ship, laughing
Into the harbour, deserting the smell of death, the lice
And the dried blood in a ridge under his collar,
Deserting Dan McGee with his head in the mouth of a cannon,
Crying, 'Goodbye boys, I've had a gutful of it,' the hand
Shaking on the Lewis gun with the blood between his fingers.

'He was wild, that boy,' the old man jabbed at my ribs,
'We were in Egypt together, the things he did!'
And I think of his wildness under that weight of earth,
My father, sardonic mouthed, whom life had ground like a pestle,
Hidden behind some general's memoirs: my mother said,
'He read such deep books. I couldn't follow them.'

There was nothing to think, nothing, except to be sorry
It had all turned out so badly, and let the old men
Unpin their RSL badges and go off home for a sleep.

'Take him,' sang the sea. 'Take him and let *him* sleep,'
Six feet of scrubby earth for the boy with the curly hair,
And the old man pottering lost in the shell-grit garden,
With the shadow of the mountain settling on his face.

FROM **RAPUNZEL IN SUBURBIA**
(1975)

Ah! Those Dead Ladies

'Come through the glass Sally,
come through the glass,
come where the dead blue ladies pass,
come through the glass Sally,
come through the glass.'

('The Chapel Perilous')

I

That house has gone
              idealised now
              like other houses.
Thumb-prints washed from curtains,
boys weep in lavatories,
water breaks on mattresses,
the garden's wild, the neighbours all complaining.
Girls marry in wet white satin
                    on the lawns,
the chlorinated pools are blue with children;
                    these fiery circles
                    woven by wistaria.

Last night, a gale:
I thought we'd go
under the Tasman Sea.
Ceilings fell on bedsteads,
              ambulances howled,
the two old sisters whinged
              all night in the attic.
The hare rose in Centennial Park
              and danced till dawn,
Henry Parkes, Diana and Hercules
sailed under the Moreton Bays
where the rape packs wait,
              to drown their girls
in the duckponds of memory...

This morning they were out,
              tending the maidenhair,
arm in arm, unshakeable as mist,
scraping the aphis off the roses.

Coming suddenly into a room,
        with chrysanthemums,
I catch them between the glass
        and open shutters.
Music brings them,
        pitifully out of tune
        by the open piano.
'They were sweet old things
        but mad.
Two sisters, a brother, parted
        how they cried!
But it ended happily,
        all loonies together
        in Ryde. It was nice for them.'

Fern baskets swing in the rain,
ivy trails on trellises,
hands touch locks smudge glass
breathes catch fingers close
together   ah!   those dead ladies.

    II

'She let all the rooms,
locked the mad one up in the shed
        to catch pneumonia.
They carried her out, feet first,
through the streaming ivy.
The old horse coughed and ran,
the imbecile drove the hearse,
        his coat tails flapping.
The landlady sat bolt upright,
        her hatpin gleamed,'
says truthful Jack
        under his caustic soda.

'Years later she came to the gate,
        hand on the latch,
        her 4 wits strayed.
"I'm going home," she said.
They sent the green cart,
the old brother crowed clapped
        wept in the windows.

"You're welcome," he said.
so she climbed in   smiling,'
        says caustic Jack
        with his tinful
                of truthful soda.

'Velia, ah! Velia,
        the witch of the wood,'
        plays the pianola
        under the pimpling rain.

By her iron bedstead
the carpets worn white in a ring,
the hare dances,
the pervert exposes himself
                in diminishing
                        circles...

'Would I not die for you
                dear if I could,'
        plays the pianola
                behind the pearling pane.

In Moncur Street

It's twenty years ago and more
since first I came to Moncur Street,
and lived with Aime and Alf among
the boarders on the second floor.

The stew was burnt, the budgie sang,
as Aime walked home the church-bells rang,
she banged the pots, ring-ding-a-ding,
she'd lost at Housie in the Spring.

But Sammy Smiles (that lovely man),
still visits her on Saturday,
Beat runs a book, and little Fay
whines in the stairwell every day
                in Moncur Street
                in Moncur Street.

Alf rose before the morning light,
and took a chopper in his hand;
he chopped and chopped in Oxford Street.
'Alf runs around without his head,
he's like a chook,' said Aime
                and sighed
for Sammy Smiles (that lovely man),

and Sunny Corner where she played
at 'Ladies' in the willow's shade.
At sunset by the empty shops
they swapped their dusty acid drops:
who lounges in the crystal air,
but Sammy Smiles, with marcelled hair!

I woke up in the darkest night,
knew all the world had caught alight.
The surf was pounding in the weather,
and Moncur Street was mine forever.
The little bat upon the stair
came out and flapped: it wasn't there,
the snapshot album turned and turned,

the stew caught fire, the budgie burned,
the pensioners at drafts and dreams,
picked bugs between their trouser seams.

And Sammy Smiles (that lovely man!)
and Aime and Alf and little Fay,
and Beat and Bert and betting slips,
the man I loved, the child I bore,
have all gone under Bondi's hills,
and will return here nevermore,
                    in Moncur Street
                    in Moncur Street.

Alf starts up his steady snore,
'Them Bondi sandhill's paved with gold,
I could've bought them for a song.'
The home brew bursts behind the door.
Aime lies upon her back and sighs:
'In Sunny Corner by the store
Sam kissed me once when I turned four.'

Dreams are deep and love is long:
she turns upon her other side.

Living Dangerously

O to live dangerously again,
meeting clandestinely in Moore Park
the underground funds tucked up between our bras,
the baby's pram stuffed with illegal lit.
We hung head down for slogans on the Bridge,
the flatbed in the shed ran ink at midnight.

Parked in the driveway, elaborately smoking,
the telltale cars, the cameras, shorthand writers.
Plans for TAKING OVER..3YRS. THE REVOLUTION.
The counter revs out gunning for the cadres.
ESCAPE along the sea shelf, wading through
            warm waters soft with blood.
WOW! WHAT A STORY!...guerrilla fighters
wear cardigans and watch it on the Box,
lapsed Party cards, and Labor's in again.
Retired, Comrade X fishes Nambucca Heads,
& Mrs Petrov, shorthand typist,
                hiding from reporters
                brings home the weekly bacon.

But   O   O   O   to live
            so dangerously again,
their stamina trousers pulling at the crutch.

Alice in a German Garden

Do you remember the garden in the watery sunlight...
Delphiniums, striped canvas swings rocking the bald-headed writers?
We dodged the shadows of ravens swooping down out of the boughs,
Searching for eyes and hearts.
The young spies struggled manfully in the flower borders,
Clutching and cocking giant Salvador Dali ears
That pulled their bodies sideways like fleshy tape-recorders
Hung upside down in the shrubbery behind our heads.

We are caught here, embedded in glass under the plastic flowers
At the foot of Heine's statue; our American voices echo
Across the borders, harsh with chain-smoking and endless coughing
In misty gardens: the thirties created us, McCarthy made us immortal,
The Cold War embalmed us; we creak in the wicker chairs
Under the linden trees in a strange climate: the high falsetto
Of the huge Negro tenor, carolling his thin German lieder
Out in the provinces, caught soliciting pretty boys
Along the Unter den Linden...it was all hushed up
For his faded little Eva, refugees out of a Faulkner mythology tale:
The drawling Southern heat, the white dust, the plaster pillars
At the end of the long oleander avenue, the rickety frame house
From a jerky movie, all lost, lost now, the black boy screaming
In the empty road, clutching his bloody genitals.
The exiles' voices float like a mockery in a second-rate light opera
Of peeling gilt and miniature velvet boxes...The Duchess is here,
The Dormouse diving his head in the priceless Sèvres teapot,
The punchbowl from Macey's shatters in rainbows on the grass,
Home movies: the Hollywood Ten unwrap their celluloid bandages,
The porch flickers with light and blood; the Red Queen
Douses her screams in the pan of the new American toilet.
'Alice, Alice will you come back next year
For the International Meeting of the Veterans of the Spanish Civil
      War?'

The motor-boat rocks – its engine cut – at the foot of the garden
Reflected twice in the water; petrol is rationed; it will never
Take us down the gleaming front of the river to Günter Grass.
The industrialists have three chins, their napkins, snowy-white,
Foam on their waistcoats; crackling green-backed dollars
They spoon pink ice cream behind the plate-glass windows.
The Nazis are howling into their microphones in Bavaria.
The glass doors of the Hotel Berolina swing open automatically
At a footfall; the heated dome of light will sweat and swarm
With faces and the swimming bite of cognac on the tongue.
The Alsatians pace endlessly up and down the borders,
The Vopos click their rifles at Checkpoint Charlie.
Why do we all keep on meeting the same characters
Like a morality play; the taxi driver who snarls
'This country is shit', the young West German who married
The East German girl, and can't go home to mother,
The silent waiter who spits his contempt on the pavement?

'Did your books get through last month,
Or did you again receive only the dust jackets?
I have complained to the Ministry of Culture.'

'My novel has been pulped, my heart beat is getting fainter,
What was the date on my last letter?'...
Oh! Alice, Alice, remember the beleaguered garden,
Remember the raven waiting in the linden tree.

Moon-Man

Stranded on the moon,
a librium dreamer in a lunar landscape,
the tabloids were full of your blurred, blown-up face,
the neat curled head, the secret animal eyes,
immolated forever in the Sea of Tranquillity.

I keep getting messages from outer space,
'Meet me at Cape Canaveral, Houston, Tullamarine.'
A telegram came through at dawn to the Dead Heart Tracking
        Station.
I wait on winter mornings in hangars
dwarfed by grounded crates like giant moths
    furred with frost.

Moon-pictures – you dance clumsily on the screen,
phosphorescent, domed, dehumanised,
    floating above the dust,
your robot voice hollow as bells.

The crowds queue for the late edition,
scan headlines avidly, their necks permanently awry,
looking for a sign, a scapegoat, a priest, a king:
the circulation is rising.

They say you have been knighted in your absence,
but those who swear they know you best,
assert you are still too radical to accept the honour.

They have sent several missions,
but at lift-off three astronauts fried,
    strapped in their webbing.
Plane-spotters on penthouse roofs
have sighted more UFOs.

Sometimes I go out at night
    to stare at the galaxies.
Is that your shadow, weightless,
    magnified in light,
man's flesh enclosed in armour,
suffering eyes in perspex looking down,
sacred and murderous from your sanctuary?

Miss Hewett's Shenanigans

They call, 'The Prince has come,'
& I swan down in astrakan & fur,
the lemon curtains blown against the light,
the scent of lilac on the balconies.
In the entrance hall
the Prince is standing
        staring at my thighs.
He mounts, how cold the marble
underneath my buttocks.
As he rides he calls me
        'whore' & 'princess'.
A platinum crooner, old as Alice Faye,
belts out bad ragtime in the empty ballroom.
The Prince, buttoning his fly,
is doing push-ups & demanding saunas.
Two giant Ghanians smile & kiss my hand.

Snow piles like roses
        up against the panes,
the waiter brings 'Ogonyok',
SINYAVSKY'S FLED & SOLZHENITSYN'S EXILED.
The lights all fail,
the electrician's pinching bulbs
from the chandeliers, shoving them
        down his shirtfront.
Outside in the dark at Lenin's tomb
they endlessly queue for weeping
        at the waxworks.
The Prince is in the Conference Hall,
listening through headphones
to a speech in seven languages.
Handsome Yugoslav colonels
discreetly try my doorknobs.
Exhausted, we sleep among carved bears
with ashtrays in their paws,
he refuses, once again, to consummate
                our marriage.

Next day we catch the Trans-Siberian
to Peking; from the observation car
we watch two wolves pacing out the train,
the Prince throws pennies to Manchurian children.
On the Great Wall he lets the wind blow
through my hair, in the Forbidden City
we listen to the clockwork nightingale.

By Aeroflot we fly in to Berlin,
the Prince will not declare his Camels
                    at Checkpoint Charlie,
(An international incident is narrowly averted.)
In the country house of Hitler's wormy mistress
we row on a lake circled with tuber roses.
The Prince, a playboy in a boater hat,
is picking the plastic flowers
                    off Heine's statue;
denouncing Nazis he pisses in the Weimar
                                    fountain,
rides with a chignoned spy
                    down Karl Marx Allee.
Tiring of this,
        we climb across the Wall,
the Vopos bow, goosestep & fire a round,
the bullets spurt,
we show our elegant heels.
In West Berlin the Prince
calls for his breakfast, on TV
Brezhnev has cancer, enters the Mayo clinic.

The Prince leafs through his autographs,
Picasso, Gandhi, Garbo, Pasternak,
calls Nabokov long distance, mounts me,
yawns, the Brandenburg Gate whirls
& explodes in the pale autumn air.
Next morning he leaves,
                    taking all my roubles.

Suffering from migraine
I enter a Retreat
among the Alps I write him
endless letters.

The corridors are full of parasites,
consumptives haemorrhage in their sleety
                              deckchairs,
in the white nights I masturbate
                    my pillows.

        An aerogramme arrives,
        'The Prince is dead!'
I take up seances,
each night we couple,
circling the empty ballroom
                    to 'Moscow Nights'.
Cockroaches rustle, my thrombosed knee
reeks of its vodka bandage,
the dust settles from the chandelier
            on his bald head...

Underneath the Arches

I wear black now,
the witch's clothes.
Portents, omens, stab me in the dark.
Old age is either pastels, twin-sets, pearls of
            gentle wisdom, or else a robe of power.

A difficult sleight of hand –
to remain vulnerable to experience,
yet closed in the black cloak of flesh.

To stand open in a wooden O
            is always risky,
but a cyclorama of small orbs, a moon,
a skyrocket or two, is never vulgar,
and cosmic imagery is right in fashion.

The impudent terror of the lady sawed in half,
for that one needs the magic nudity –
34   24   34.

If you didn't drop dead in the Tiv,
            a Marcus *Girl*,
suffocated in a tight skin of gilded flesh,
mourned by Lennie Lower, Mo and Cine-
sound,
don't haunt the massage parlours:
G-strings don't snap on hairy terrors.

But power is something else:
to write a poem
Dame Edith Sitwell
bade the London jackhammers cease,
and Nellie Melba (with insomnia)
stopped the Town Hall clock in Bendigo.

Dissolving in a spotlight
            keep your cool
with a pack of tarot cards
and jiggery-pokery behind a screen.
Gentlemen may remove any garment consistent with decency.
Ladies may remove any garment consistent with charm.

Picasso's 'Girl With Dove'

The girl in the blue dress with the dove in her arms
is standing forever in the curve of the hall.
Nobody notices her there:
she has merged into the curtain's shadow,
or the strange blue light that comes
from the pine tree outside the open window.
But I am always conscious of her, her cropped head bent
tenderly over the dove, her milky eyes
fixed on me with gentle accusation.

Darby and Joan

If we'd grown old together
Our hatreds honed to bone,
We'd have shared a poisoned afghan robe.
God bless our hearth and home.

If we'd grown old together,
the arsenic you always thought was in your porridge,
would I have dropped it in?
On either side of the hearth
would we have rocked into oblivion,
savouring the cyanide pellet in the Robur tea,
the hemlock floating in the clear soup from Meals on Wheels?
The unlit gas full on
the loaded gun triggered from the broom cupboard,
straight between your eyes;
the thick blue air
stuffed with *Sunday Suns* under the doors and window-sills,
while you took 40 winks.

All those games of hide-and-seek in draughty rooms,
giddy with hate, to fall one day
in the empty hall, and stink like carrion.
Would you have gone on playing clown to my straight man,
bony on the congoleum,
accusing me of kinky infidelities
with old great-uncles building rat's nest cubbies in our yard?
Or perhaps they'd put us side by side in curly
wicker chairs, unravelling on some secluded verandah
in Eventide,
scorpions in a sunny bottle,
to sting ourselves to death,
And then the predestined end;
stone-throwing boys break the glass dome
furred with waxy flowers:
'Beloved wife and husband'.

I take our grandchild up,
feeling the generations tug my arms,
trace your features and your lineaments
                      through twelve years separation.
Low to high fortune, that's a comedy.
GOD BLESS OUR HEARTH AND HOME.

Look, Look I Have Come Home

I left you, but I always meant
to come back: you forever frozen,
waiting behind the *Herald*
in the bed. I never thought you'd go.
The grass would grow higher, blot out the glass,
the date palm brush the gutters,
the trains rush by to Newcastle & Wynyard.
On the lawn next door a man was always hammering
a glider, it never got off the ground.
One day I'd walk back,
see the shadow of the sunflower on the wall,
its round and furry centre eaten out by bees.
Yesterday I rode past in a train,
saw the home units, all the car yards
strewn with plastic banners.
'Five Ways' the signpost said,
Five Ways to death and madness.
Behind that door my Madame Tussaud's waxworks,
the blue heeler whimpers at your hand.

Anniversary

Driving back after midnight,
black streets, empty asphalt, wind.
Suddenly a rain of yellow leaves.
They lay in drifts over the wheel hubs,
clogging the windscreen wipers...confetti?
We were driving home from our wedding,
an old shoe bumped behind us, full of leaves.

Island and Forest

Islands rise out of the sea,
ceremonial, round,
Illyria has two weeping palaces
and a shipwrecked shore.

Crouched under a rock,
your lost child at your side,
eyes dark with dolphins and fishes,
your nets come dripping from the tide.

The island is full of noise,
the boy girdles the earth
with a circling rod of fishes,
but the man stands still in the surf,
the pearls moist in his eyes,
Caliban-Ferdinand-Prospero,
the beast is exorcised,
and the maimed Fisher King by the wreck,
casting his net in the sea,
brings the albatross out by the neck.

Islands are magical rings,
round green circles of fire,
lions roar in the Forest of Arden,
asses bray in the midsummer woods.
We stand deprived in the dark,
to the receding wash of the wave,
Miranda and Ferdinand move
chess pieces in a luminous cave.

Before we break the staff,
and sink into the sea,
here by the southern ocean
I pray for you
on your island.
                    pray for me.

Grave Fairytale

I sat in my tower, the seasons whirled,
the sky changed, the river grew
and dwindled to a pool.
The black Witch, light as an eel,
laddered up my hair
to straddle the window-sill.

She was there when I woke, blocking the light,
or in the night, humming, trying on my clothes.
I grew accustomed to her; she was as much a part of me
as my own self; sometimes I thought, 'She *is* myself!'
a posturing blackness, savage as a cuckoo.

There was no mirror in the tower.

Each time the voice screamed from the thorny garden
I'd rise and pensively undo the coil,
I felt it switch the ground, the earth tugged at it,
once it returned to me knotted with dead warm birds,
once wrapped itself three times around the tower – the tower quaked.
Framed in the window, whirling the countryside
with my great net of hair I'd catch a hawk, a bird, and once a bear.
One night I woke, the horse pawed at the walls,
the cell was full of light, all my stone house
suffused, the voice called from the calm white garden, 'Rapunzel'.
I leant across the sill, my plait hissed out and spun like hail;
he climbed, slow as a heartbeat, up the stony side,
we dropped together as he loosed my hair,
his foraging hands tore me from neck to heels:
the witch jumped up my back and beat me to the wall.

Crouched in a corner I perceived it all,
the thighs jack-knifed apart, the dangling sword thrust home,
pinned like a specimen – to scream with joy.

I watched all night the beasts unsatisfied
roll in their sweat, their guttural cries
made the night thick with sound.
Their shadows gambolled, hunch-backed, hairy-arsed,
and as she ran four-pawed across the light,
the female dropped coined blood spots on the floor.

When morning came he put his armour on,
kissing farewell like angels swung on hair.
I heard the metal shoes trample the round earth about my tower.
Three times I lent my hair to the glowing prince,
hand over hand he climbed, my roots ached,
the blood dribbled on the stone sill.
Each time I saw the framed-faced bully boy sick with his triumph.

The third time I hid the shears,
a stab of black ice dripping in my dress.
He rose, his armour glistened in my tears,
the convex scissors snapped,
the glittering coil hissed, and slipped through air to undergrowth.
His mouth, like a round O, gaped at his end,
his finger nails ripped out, he clawed through space.
His horse ran off flank-deep in blown thistles.
Three seasons he stank at the tower's base.
A hawk plucked out his eyes, the ants busied his brain,
the mud-weed filled his mouth, his great sword rotted,
his tattered flesh-flags hung on bushes for the birds.

Bald as a collaborator I sit walled in the thumb-nosed tower,
wound round three times with ropes of autumn leaves.
And the witch...sometimes I idly kick
a little heap of rags across the floor.
I notice it grows smaller every year.

FROM **GREENHOUSE**
(1979)

Madame Bovary

In the village ghetto   hand to mouth
the funereal carriage spokes
flash by the park the bridge across
the harbour smiling in the courtyard
on the balcony smiling   the camera clicks
the mirrored cadenced voices
faking it   Bovary the sentimental arsenic
lady   is she the one you met   the one
you knew so well?

the rose bowls full of early summer's petals
on glass tabletops she leaves love-letters
the drapes looped back   the autumn light
falls in great shafts through the floorlength windows
outside under the birch trees a girl abandoned
her black cloak scuffs the leaves
obliterating everything   ...

the garden's empty   in the last light
between the avenues twin horses plunge
the carriage rocks without a driver
running through bare trees the whipbirds in
the topmost branches torment her
back to childhood where a room waits by a river
waterfalled in light   ...

flee from this garden in the house of sighs
love rocks the bed she shared with many lovers
a note left on a pillow barefoot through golden gorse
she drives with one dark man & then another
the husband waits   the children cry   alone
she takes the powder   her back arches in parody
the grey brothers stand at her right shoulder
the one you meet   the one you knew so well
Bovary   the sentimental arsenic lady.

Green Jack & Mother Gloom

In the locked garden in the ominous wood
cricket owl & cockerel cry
Burn the effigy of Mother Gloom

She said   I will sit upright   I will never
go to bed then I cannot die

crops & restless rooms   faint murmurous voices
      infinite space   this was the centre
of all my earthly hopes & joys –

I had a son half-man & half-beast
a green man covered head-to-foot in leafy branches
Jack-in-the-Green   Jack-in-the-Bush
master of fire   charmer   practitioner
of the Occult   we copulated in the fields
to make sure of a good Spring.

As long as the king was maimed no crops were sown
no child was born no meadows turned to green
I hanged myself on the curtain rod   I don't believe
the dead return because they were loved or happy.

Happy is the corpse that the rain rains on
Happy is the bride that the sun shines on

pass through   the arch   the cycle   & the swan

Psyche's Husband

He is the Monster-husband who comes
to Psyche in the darkness of her wish-palace.
ROBERT DUNCAN: The Truth & Life of Myth

In the darkness of the myth-palace I sit waiting
the feast is laid the tapers lit   the musak plays
the crow sharpens & taps a beak on the iron cradle
along the marble halls I can hear paws dragging
a giant shadow falls
the baby cries with the wind in its christening robes
& the beast is upon me
the stink from its snout   its sad pig eyes
its fur ripples along my skin
kiss me   it sobs   melodious-voiced   *kiss me*

I run shrieking through the palace
as I snatch up the child the crow pecks at my wrists
the carpet lifts with the draughts under the doors
the air-conditioner   humming   is set up high
I look back only once
there is a toad with a horned head
sadly plopping down the stairs behind me
kiss me   it croaks   *kiss me*
the crow drinks my blood on the doormat
that spells   WELCOME

now I live in the woodcutter's cottage
nodding in the peaceful kingdom
sometimes I hear the crow squawking
as it scans the canopy of leaves above my head
the toad squats & snaps in the marshes
the glamorous roar of the beast hums under my feet

my son with the beast's snout the toad's horn
& the crow's claw snuffles for acorns
along the floor of the rain-forest
kiss me   he snorts   *kiss me.*

Anniversary

Death is in the air –

today is the anniversary of his death in October
(he would have been thirty-one)
I went home to High Street
& couldn't feed the new baby
my milk had dried up
so I sat holding him numbly
looking for the soft spot on the top of his head
while they fed me three more librium
you're only crying for yourself he said
but I kept on saying *It's the waste I can't bear.*

All that winter we lived
in the longest street in the world
he used to walk to work in the dark
on the opposite side of the street
somebody always walked with him but they never met
he could only hear the boots
& when he stopped they stopped.

The new baby swayed in a canvas cot lacing his fingers
I worried in case he got curvature of the spine
Truby King said a baby needed firm support
he was a very big bright baby
the cleaner at the Queen Vic said every morning
you mark my words that kid's been here before.

The house was bare & cold with a false gable
we had no furniture only a double mattress
on the floor a big table & two deal chairs
each morning I dressed the baby in a shrunken jacket
& caught the bus home to my mother's to nurse the child
who was dying   the house had bay windows
hidden under fir trees smothered in yellow roses
the child sat dwarfed at the end of the polished table
pale as death in the light of his four candles
singing *Little Boy Blue.*

I pushed the pram to the telephone box
I'm losing my milk I told her   *I want to bring him
home to die*   *Home* she said   *you left
home a long time ago to go with that man.*

I pushed them both through the park
over the dropped leaves (his legs were crippled)
a magpie swooped down black out of the sky
& pecked his forehead   a drop of blood splashed on
his wrist   he started to cry

It took five months & everybody was angry
because the new baby was alive & cried for attention
pollen sprinkled his cheeks under the yellow roses.

When he died it was like everybody else
in the public ward with the screens around him
the big bruises spreading on his skin
his hand came up out of the sheets *don't cry*
he said   *don't be sad*
I sat there overweight in my Woolworth's dress
not telling anybody in case they kept him alive
with another transfusion –

        Afterwards I sat by the gas fire
in my old dressing-gown turning over the photographs
wondering why I'd drunk all that stout
& massaged my breasts every morning to be
        a good mother.

The Mandelstam Letters

You took away all the oceans and all the room.
You gave me my shoe-size in earth with bars around it.
Where did it get you? Nowhere.
You left me my lips, and they shape words, even in silence.

OSIP MANDELSTAM
(Voronezh, 1935)

First Voronezh Letter

My goldfinch I'll cock my head
together we'll look at the world:

Voronezh, December 1936

Catching wild birds   at the bird auction
& selling them as songsters   I bought a caged goldfinch
the bird my own likeness   I order it to live.
Nightingales larks & goldfinches fall from the sky
drab little birds   compensated by song.
This goldfinch is kept in a cage   it is not allowed in the forest
     glades with their barbed wire
     entanglements.
Don't talk about it or it may all begin to happen;
I lost my whitehandled walking-stick after writing *The Patriarch*,
the travelling rug that covered me fell apart after the line,
you will cover me with it as with a military flag when I die
the apartment for which we fought so hard did not survive
                the poem,
         our goldfinch was eaten by the cat…
Akhmatova, my Notebooks!   Exiled, cast out by my tribe
I am your fellow traveller   my lips are bluer…
moving my lips at Voronezh   I dictate my verse to you.

The horses' hoofs on the roadway are full of water like memory,
nobody speaks to us, we are not invited into homes,
         not recognised in public places;
we rent a room in the house of the seamstress on a hill above
the river   a tumbledown wooden place sunken
into the ground;   in front of the seamstress' house
        boys toboggan to the very edge.

(In Moscow I wore a wretched priest's coat of motheaten racoon,
long and ungainly as a cassock, witness to my bourgeois ideology;
Prishvin used it as a mattress on the Tvereskoi Boulevard;
when his primus stove exploded it stifled the flames,
      the last bits of racoon fur were scorched away.)

Are you a priest or a General, Mister?
shout the tobogganing boys   *A little of both*
               by train and steamship
          my sub-conscious so full it must spill over
I stroll in my imagination round the Baptistry in Florence,
I have just been on a secret trip to the Crimea,
I draw strength from Autumn and the bitter cold of Winter,
these things cannot be taken away.
My key poems are like tuning forks, bright nostalgic journeys,
this is also a journey   death   my coffin
in a wooden overcoat carried through the streets of Moscow,
lid open   snowflakes falling   unclosed eyelids
                     I will abandon earth,
the vendettas of the Writers' Organisations, old leaders
perishing devoured from above: in the local branch of the secret
                     police
they turn the files like contracted centuries, turning aside
                     from me
their embarrassed eyes: I am turned into wood...
               Akhmatova   preserve my speech!

Second Voronezh Letter

1937 is close at hand: on the River Don we heard over the radio
the beginning of the Terror in the summer of '36.
Kirov's murderers are discovered, the Trials are in preparation.
Lying in bed, or Mohammedans by the iron stove, we sit for days
　　　awaiting our fate;
we lie quite still in our houses pretending oblivion.
I am like a child closing its eyes or a bird dropping its head under
　　　its wing;
all the singers are exiled from Leningrad; the spy next door,
with the rank of General, copies out my poems on his typewriter.
Everyday I compose a sonnet in my head, on Tuesday I said enough
　　　to get ten years,
we drop our petitions in boxes, nobody unfolds them.
The Commandant interviews me in an office composed of doors.
The order is　　*to isolate and preserve.*
When the archives are one day thrown open no witnesses will come
　　　forth;
Akhmatova purses her lips to say *No,*
Antigone immolated in her self-made tomb, struggling for breath.
The Film Studios, the Faculties of Literature, Philosophy and
　　　Economics, swarm with spies,
they loiter for hours in front of Akhmatova's lodgings, yet the desire
　　　to live
is insuperable.

I will pick up my pencil like Fedin;
(Fedin in the elevator at the Hotel Berolina
discoursing in French with Neruda, *Never a day without a line !)*

I will write an ode with a rope around my neck.
My 3 year exile ends in '37; a poem buzzes in my head.
I transcribe it into the Second Voronezh Notebook.

Third Moscow Letter

After 3 years Moscow is an hallucination;
an empty apartment, beds, curtains, shelves, a handful of books.
Do you remember the apartment in Furmanov Street in the summer
    of '33,
the pink-cheeked Chekhist treating us to hard candy in a tin box,
    Where do you keep your Marxist classics?
In this century of illusory activity, illusionary love affairs, hanging
    on grimly
to our living space, nobody reads our letters, or takes us by the hand.
I wander the streets alone, half out of my mind, we have some
    possessions,
a bucket, a frying pan, a lamp and a flatiron; we are Soviet citizens,
afraid of unexpected visitors, cars stopping outside the house, the
    sound
of elevators at night: in an inexplicable state of calm
I believe my life is secure, everybody is intolerably late, nobody has
    watches,
trains and buses run erratically, the mattress,
for fear of bedbugs, is set across the hall, burying our heads
in the pillows we try to pretend we are peacefully asleep.
In case I am arrested in the street I carry *The Divine Comedy*.

Akhmatova and I have a private vocabulary; I once made friends
with Mayakovsky in Petersburg; arriving in Kiev
with a wicker basket crammed with poems and my mother's letters,
the Crimean soldiers broke the lock, used the paper to roll cigarettes;
I put together my second book from memory:
how can a young man imagine his scribblings may one day be
    valuable?
In those days we never thought a man might die and his memory
    with him.
Where are my friendly listeners? Have they all gone into the camps?

A trunk bought in Munich, plastered with foreign labels, rough
        drafts of poems,
letters and essays, useless paper money left over from Kerensky,
        this is my archive
everything is in it.   Akhmatova delivered Gumilyov's archive by
        sledge.
As the feathers flew from the Jewish cushions in Deniken's pogroms
        in Kiev, everything
conspires to sweep us away, poor scraps of paper like foam   whirl
        totally
isolated buried under snow
O my confiscated poems! People will keep my work for me sewn
        into cushions,
stuck inside saucepans and shoes, make copies,
passing from hand to hand, hidden in a thousand secret places,
        remembered,
forgotten, human life grows cheaper
my memory is not as good as it used to be our dialogue is over for
        the time being
yet it is dangerous to stop talking, we might forget
how to do it.   *I have been arrested! for God's sake*
burn everything   disperse and fly like leaves

Fourth Exile's Letter

I come home to find they have cancelled my permit to live in the
        city,
expelled from Moscow, months in the Lubianka.
It's spring, I've sold my leather-jacket now I wear an old coat made
        of dog's skin.
Along the Yaroslavl railroad the prisoners are taken to Siberia.

I live in Strunina in the 105 kilometre zone, we eat wild berries in
        the woods, we live like hunted animals in the taiga.
She spins the yarn and memorises my verses...

I got into hot water in the offices of *Izvestia*.
They said, *Do you know what happens after you write a poem like that?*
        Three men come for you in uniform.
We live beyond the 100th kilometre, sitting out things in the these
        savage times.
Moscow draws us like a magnet, stranded for one night in the
        Forbidden City we missed the last train back to Kalinin.
In the streets of Moscow in my dogskin jacket I am taken for an
        exile.
There is a biting wind on the bridge across the Volga, the wind of
        persecution and exile.
We trudge along to our rented room on the edge of town,
the streets are impassable with mud and snow, our landlady serves
        us tea from a samovar with home-made jam,
the lamps are lit before the icon, we read *Pravda*, have concerts on
        the phonograph Dvorak Mussorgsky the Brandenburg
        Concerto,
we are part of the hare-brained upper crust, we lack the will to live,
let people up top meddle and murder each other, go to the devil
        in their own sweet way,
we made a revolution   but nobody asked us to. Don't cry, we'll
        be like the saints.

We spent two months in the Writers' Rest Home in Samatikha,
      baffled by such duplicity.
There are phone calls, enquiries about our health, we even have
      ice cream on the 1st of May!
we live in a quaint forest hut, totally isolated, we seem to be very
      big fish indeed.
They are beginning to look after us   do you think
                 we have fallen into a trap?
In the morning somebody knocks quietly on the door.
Two men in uniform say *Come with us. You'll have to go all the way*
      to Siberia to mend your ways.

Everything moves so smoothly, the sleigh with the sheepskin rugs
      waiting to keep us warm,
we are treated like guests of honour, it is a very cold March and the
      pine trees crackle with frost.
The Party is an inverted church mirrored
      in the Kremlin towers.

Last Letters from the Transport Camp
Vitoraya Rechka, near Vladivostok

Let me tell you about the last days of Osip Mandelstam.
You will go to the Post Office at Nikita Gate, and be handed a parcel,
      ADDRESSEE DEAD, you will need no witnesses, learn of it
      only by hearsay.

The train travelled east, I lay in my bunk covered with a blanket,
starving myself to death, will they inject me with rabies as 'socially
      dangerous'?

The loft is lit by a candle, sitting with criminals, a man
with a grey beard in a yellow jacket recites his verses,
clothes freeze in the air, rattle like sheets of tin.
Was I the demented old man of seventy, nicknamed the Poet,
reading Petrarch by the light of the campfire, called away to eat
      kasha?

A line from one of my poems is scratched on the prison wall: *Am I*
real and will death really come?

The date of my death was given, the cause heart failure, but what
    is death but a failure of the heart.
Nobody washed my body or put me into the grave.

My first book was Stone, and my last will be stone also.
We have done away with a great poet said Fadeyev, drinking a toast,
but every poet should have 12 volumes with gilt edges & write like Walter
    Scott.

In the Writers' Apartments with their labradorite entrances it is like
    doomsday,
The floor where they put you depends on your standing.
Some are trampled underfoot like demons, some have their praises
    sung.
They are opening bank accounts, buying new furniture, writing sordid
    novels (Fedin's apartment is crammed with mahogany),
talent and cynicism make useful bedfellows.
They have spent all their lives at desks, suffering from insomnia,
Sleep won't come; on a sled covered with straw
Marina Tsvetayeva, her neck snapped like a string whirls through
    the Moscow nights;
Akhmatova purses her lips: We were two little girls
in white starched dresses crying out: *We don't want to go to the*
    Orphanage, we want to go Home.

What silly little girls! We must send them away before it is too late.
No record! Next! says the face behind the window.

Nobody remembers Mandelstam in the new Moscow nowadays.

The past was an historical necessity, everybody is a candidate for
    prison and death.

Woe   woe   fear the snare and the pit cries Gumilyov
Live while you can   and we will see says Mandelstam.

Sydney Postscript

Let's start as though we were stretched / on the headsman's block,
you and I / on the other side of seventy years   (Moscow, November 1933)

This is our fate	the	stoney faces
Mayakovsky's bedbugs	crawlers	in rented rooms
Christs with dimpled female knees	hang	over the painful beds
the women lie visionary	in rows	cataract eyes ablaze
led by nurses	line up	at the cracked handbasins
lift dazed faces	listening	to the sound of wheelchairs
pneumatic tyres	creak	on worn linoleum
glass-eyed men	moan	in the wards all night
the women stride the balcony	stroking	their cancerous breasts
tomorrow they will wear	silicone	under their jumpers
the soles of my shoes	worn through	from composing poetry
I run down the hospital stairs	hold	the dead child in the heart
tonguetied guttersnipes	make copies of	my verses
pay me	testify	'we'll hear no more of this!'
I am sending my poems	to the literary mags	bookshops no longer stock them
poems are illegal	poems are	obliterated
one of the accusations	against you	you circulated your verses
in this country I live	only for the present	a little serenity
it is unforgivably vain	unforgivable	to compare ourselves.

Beata Beatrix

I read the legend of myself from an enormous book.
JOURNALS OF ANAÏS NIN

1

Out in the garden my daughter says to me,
Trees & women burn!
The shadows lattice on the courtyard floor.
Late afternoon...petals spill from the rose arbour,
the wild orange scatters,
hail storms whiten the streets.

No letters & no love
spin silk for your coffin.

2

Under the wild orange, drinking ice-cubes
        reading Kazantzakis,
why shouldn't I be happy?
A week has passed, your letter hasn't come.
For the first time you haven't written.
Why is it so important after thirty years?
Three weeks ago we were resurrected,
I watched through the window, hiding behind
        my typewriter,
drinking diluted whisky with a beating heart,
marvelling that the only difference was in your grey hair.

Now you have another icon to drive past
        on your way to work,
barefooted, in a blue dress, turned to placid stone.
The air is full of wild orange, amorous as love,
        drinking ice-cubes, reading Kazantzakis,
why shouldn't I be happy?
The only difference is in your grey hair...
        but   still   the letter hasn't come.

3

What do I want with a 7-roomed house
             & a conservatory!
All I need is a tin trunk like Mandelstam.

At Sackville I lived in the editor's house,
             high-nosed   disdainful   freakish!
with a typewriter & my unyielding art:
the old man's hat & stick laid out by the fireplace,
             the cat on the step   it is evening
             they are still calling to each other,
the phone rings through the empty house:
Beatrice are you well?   Dante, my love, take care!
you have swung hundreds of light bulbs in the garden
             so I won't be frightened,
at dawn the house floats on a raft of mist
             across the river...
trees burst into flame   life is purgatory
             how long can we keep on burning?

4

I sit in a state of grace in my high-backed wicker armchair
you watch my window waiting for the light to go out,
the French doors open before me   lead me onto
             the balcony
the Harbour illuminated   the Communists holding
             a meeting for La Pasionaria
the river dances   laps on my bedroom ceiling.

I am writing an autobiography, crystal-gazing my childhood
eyeglasses without a glass half a book half a toy
             bird-cages   broken records   an earring
a single glove   repetition   monotony
the austere joys of work
all the fairytales are possible for me
I have written a love poem
I am lonely   my friends are no longer sufficient
             do not abandon me...

in life one must accept the limitations
             no one has ever loved an adventurous woman

Father & Daughter

I can still see you reading the rain-gauge
under the almond trees
where we buried the wax doll that winter.

We played at horses whinnying down the lawn
lay in the Willys Knight by the cubby-house
re-enacting *Death & the Maiden.*

When we dug up the wax doll with her melted face
she had pride of place in the empty playroom
              victim of an acid attack.

That summer you had rheumatics so badly
you hobbled on two broomsticks
           to the Great Fire
the car-lights swerving down the hills
              & we remembered the neighbours...

When we left
           turning away from the iron gate
                rimed with frost
the Dutchman stood in the road
           spinning his hat in his hands
Goodbye old friend & neighbour.

We were going to run horses
           on the forty acres...

Swinging in the hammock listening to the yarns
the great talkers on the jarrah verandahs
my mother's green dress luminous in the dark
the whey-faced ewes baaing to the moon
somewhere a tractor revving up
the steam train   in the siding
           When the Armistice was signed that steam train
           came over the paddocks playing Yankee Doodle.

The clearing always smells green in retrospect
the foal's coat rimmed in light
             its forelegs trembling
you put your finger to my lips & held my hand

Too light for the plough you said
             Can I have it then? you nodded
& sold it to the Dutchman for a sulky horse.

Driving through Day's paddock down the track
made by McGonnigal on a bender
             (they always called him Jesus)
Jack Baxter's stable   lurches through the rain
Joe Swannel's cart-wheel   wobbles up ahead
Polly of the Circus   at the picture-show
in the Town Hall Max Montesole
             strangles Desdemona   the Lark Bros. sing
                   An 'am an egg & an onion
       at the RSL
country women waltz in green shawls with runny roses
Princess Marina has married the Duke of Kent
the Greek's wife celebrates with a lime-juice spider
over the rooftops with Edna the half-caste girl

There's blood on your pants
             you better tell your mother.

On the pub corner arguing politics
with Cecil Elsegood the Country Party member
my hair twines round your waistcoat button
the street runs in my tears you haven't noticed.

The Monday brothers swagger past the Co-op
shearers in their bell-bottoms
             home from jail.

Under the almond trees
Lou Fuller the clearer's son
gave me a Chinese burn
out in the sleepout
in my blue silk dress
he pressed me between his thighs
when he went away
he left his holey felt hat
hanging on the back of the door
I kept staring at it
(remembering how we raced
through the creek-bed
& I tossed my hair
the beak in my side)
till my mother noticed
& put it under the copper.

My grandmother plants the snapdragons
        she won't see
my grandfather smokes in the garden
        by the hollyhocks
my mother irons lazy-daisies
        till the pattern comes through

Hinkler fell into the sea
Bradman's LBW on the crystal set
        singing
when the moon shines over the cowshed
you carry me up the path between the fig trees.

I smash the cheval mirror
on the autumn-toned carpet
playing *Charge of the Light Brigade*
white-starred horses wheel through the rainy dark
the merry-go-round creaks
        by Yealering salt lake...
half a league   half a league

you are reading the rain-gauge
        under the almond trees.

Summer Solstice: 2

It is the miraculous summer
but who will share it
the hawk   the transfigured night
the crow in the garden
flapping around about death
a subtle & sable lover.

Dive down holding the breath
in the chill lake water
goannas bask on the bank
the watersnake slips out of reach
beneath my feet the stringybarks drown
float out with the tide under the bridge
the light above & the night below
to the saltwater river
the sky   the banks   the dark unconscious
lead to warm water   sleep & the fish
feeding blind in the shallows
the gulls cross-stitching the reef

I see the Seal   huge as a dream
lying on her side   stranded   between two black rocks
the surf pounding

stench of the Seal   her dry barnacled skin
heaving with flies   the opaque eyes
blown   fringed with lashes

I stand at the neap tide & pray for a storm
to take her out
through the rocks to the foam
where the sea-wrack races
over the sand let her ride home
to the deep places that have no naming

her shadow falls on the land
I turn   I don't look back   there is
        no claiming.

The Labyrinth

1

I carry the mirror
        into the labyrinth
        to face the Cybele
        to fight the Minotaur
locked in their lair

the lurching monster lies
        with the Ancestress
beasts couple snakes birds bears
        rove in the dark
youths spit out olive seeds
        in the Cretan sunlight
Cybele cuts off their cods
        to hang for trophies

the labyrinth is a puzzle   a maze
        where you might get lost
what will I find there in the room
        without a window?
the Sybil in a glass bell
        the test-tube baby
babbling forth prophecies
blurred visions   misty rain
        unrealisable loves...

you arrive soft-footed out of the Spring
Nureyev cheekbones   blue shirt
        faded jeans
disguised as love
carrying a white camellia down Bishop's walk
I stand in front of the boatsheds in the rain
the city burns behind me tumbling into the sea
you did not really abandon me
        you simply tried to save your life.

I make up my husband's bed   silk-sheeted
                    slippery as blood
the staghounds wait in the ute
                         with the yellow sticker
the boat without a motor is stalled in the lane
at Bajool they danced all night
with the streamers falling into the cane
10 feet   ice-green   their tits jumping out
            of their dresses
while he sat on the hill
                    & watched the schoolhouse burn
will you ever reach the harbour
steering your boat through waterless streets?
the sea has an infinite loneliness
          mermaids grow cold-hearted
solitude is not just a cabin in the woods.

2

Wake me from my dream & hand in hand
          like the first children
we will steal out of the garden   taking with us
      the illuminated places
(someone has left 21 loveletters
          in the drawer of the room next-door)
the rain falls in the courtyard
               it must be Autumn
the red leaves knock against the French windows
I think we are the last people left alive
          in the world

but the children run out suddenly
laughing into the frame of Antonioni's garden
I cannot bear the passing of things
under the arches with the lamps gleaming like operas
Operas of Death   Operas of Hope
wearing dark glasses smoking gold-tipped cigarettes
I ride past in a black Mercedes
          a female Al Capone   seeking
a miracle   seeking the love
that will try once more   lost sounds

lost colours   the curtain of the sea
the circle of empty waiting that never closes
above the clouds you are passing over the city

staring at your own reflection in the aircraft window.

3

I come back to the same garden   timidly
                pushing open the door
& walk through a city of statues   heroes & lions
angels & gargoyles impaled in the fountain's heart
                haloed in spray   frozen-lipped
astride the towers reading from books of stone
the garden is closed in infinity
if you look through a narrow window
you can photograph a girl reading under a clothesline
a phosphorescent child with an ideal self
                who is always beside her
through the eyes of that child I still look
at the world   a doll lying in a trunk
                with washed-out blue eyes the hollow notes
of the pianola   the flash of a gold ring
the snapping of gilt shirt-studs   the nightlight
casting gigantic shadows   my mother
                        in a calico nightgown
holding the poison bottle in her hand
                I was always such a comedienne hoarding
the past   I am afraid you will only inherit bric-a-brac
from me   pressed flowers   broken hairbrushes
threaded with grey-blonde hairs   bad paintings
scribbled manuscripts   remnants of Brussels lace
how will you distribute my belongings amongst you?
I have pursued these imagined images for 50 years
searching through the corridors of dreams
                the ceaseless fateful crowds   only
to find at the corner where you turn without volition
the same remembered face   preserved intact
                the gesture of dismissal.

The labyrinth lengthens   what remains?   love!
the face in the faceless throng
the remembered voice the one who gave you nothing
the forlorn struggle for dominance
                    without guilt

there is a sad woman   you keep leaving
pushed over a cliff in a wheelchair
                    whose brakes have failed.

4

I look in the mirror   my hair turns white overnight

I must break the glass that reflects
            the single image
        Bird in cage can't sing
                    said Ezra
in the Garden of Art there is knowledge
            & revelation
when I die will you make a flute out of my bones?
until then my uncompleted self goes on
            accumulating the world
even when the mirror shatters it's no solution
the thread of the past can never be broken
the bull behind my back swinging his pizzle
the beast is garlanded   the Cretan girls toss on the horn
            the cock
I face the Minotaur   the moon turns on
                    my forehead
I stand in a planetarium whirling with stars.

FROM **ALICE IN WORMLAND**
(1987)

From The Alice Poems

4

Under the swallows' nests
her grandmother lay in the sleepout
calling on God
her pupil turning milky

in the kerosene box bookcase
the Swiss Family Robinson
battled   the   giant anacondas
in the sepia photograph
mad Uncle Harry stood with the brothers
let out of the barred room
to squint at sunlight

her father drove the poison cart
like Kemal Ataturk
a khaki handkerchief fixed to his digger's hat
profile coin-stamped against the whitening sky
the racehorse goannas tore up & down the orchard.

Alice had six brothers
one lived in the silo   one in the sheepfeeder
one was a blind albino building crooked fences
one peed from the chaffhouse window
in shirt tails scratching himself
only Jack & Bob were normal
living in ruined houses along the road to York.

Playing doctors she hit Marjory Day
with the flogging hammer
a blue lump rose on her forehead
& she didn't come back to play
but there was a girl called Alma
in the wardrobe mirror who smiled
like a demon
& always understood her.

5

her grandfather was a window dresser
at The Bon Marche
he swaggered to Lodge to ride the goat
naked   a gold watch bounced on his belly
his Willys Knight bucked on the country roads
till he hit a white gum

her father was a carriage builder
like Henry Lawson
he drove the Twin City tractor
battling his migraine

her mother had change of life at 35
haemorrhaging into the frayed towels
on the leatherette sofa
she tacked a sign over Alice's bed
I must not tell lies against my mother

her grandmother took her to sit
on the wheatbags   the evenings
were full of bats   she told stories
about Mrs Love
who stood on the right hand of God
& loved all his orphan children

at night they sat round the kitchen table
eating mutton roasts on the linen tablecloth
waiting for the Albany Doctor
to blow up from the creek
they could hear it roaring
in the line of salmon gums
Alice hung head down watching the world spin
I'm a changeling   she cried
I don't belong with them

she imagined they'd found her
under the rhubarb plants
swaddled   glistening with frost
like an afterbirth
but she was wrong

the blood of them all swam in her
she was caught in the web of their history
like the tarantula
hanging from the chaffhouse rafter
waiting to reel her in.

From The Nim Poems

1

So Alice invented Nim
                (the sinister boy)
or thought she did
she heard the owl scream
& the cricket cry
like them he was her creature
& drunk with power said
Why I can make him live
                or make him die.

2

In her secret garden
under the hump of the hill
she lives her magic life
with Ida Rentoul Outhwaite's
Elves and Fairies
sheep carcasses in calico
blood-spotted shroud the verandahs
where the timber blurs
Grimm's giant flexes his whirlwind biceps
dry paddocks darken into green
the flag above the creekbed island
                bleaches yellow.

In the playroom the old dolls sit nodding
the mallee roots spin in their china eyeballs
a helmeted Apollo gleams on the pressed iron ceiling

but in the garden nothing alters
ladies' fingers ripen   larkspurs put on bells
the puffballs stand at 4 o'clock
until Nim comes   a shadow on the shivery grass
hanging between the sun & the round hill
a falcon on his wrist a white owl on his shoulder
she sees his doomed face waver at the bottom of the well

the sky darkens with locusts
the dry scratch of wings
                             & the jaws working
hand in hand they fly
Alice & Nim, the falcon & the white owl
                            from the blackened garden.

3

After the locust plague
Nim often came
to creep at dusk & weep
in her blackened garden
the hooded falcon buckled
at his wristbone
the white owl hooting
through the air
a moon with a ring rose up
behind the chaffhouse
the Italian fed the team
singing *La Paloma*
ropes of saliva swung
from their champing jaws
he dreamed of 100 French letters
hidden in the stable
the tin lizzie waiting
to rattle him into town
the stallion kicked his stall
the curled rams stamped
their horns caught
in the barbed fences
the sheep itched & rotted
on the bare hills

Come out   sobbed Nim.

4

Alice turning eleven
watching the blood trickle
between her thighs onto the warm boards
the woodbugs investigated it
for touching myself on the woodheap
I must be going to die she thought
& rolled over staring at the golden light
between the boards until her eyes ached
waiting to die   but Nim said
Alice   that's wonderful
now we can have a baby

5

You can't swim   the blood
will run up to your brain
          & you'll go mad
said her mother flapping about
like a black Orpington
          in the shallow ocean.
Between the prickly bushes
          & the peppermint trees
Alice ran through the sand dunes
                    shaking

to the cubby house
behind the creeper curtain
a tramp lay sleeping
Bottom on the green moss
braying under the knottygobbles
          with his fly open.

6

She swelled & swelled all winter
but nobody noticed
her father laughed
Alice is getting fat
she couldn't run

& she hated it
when the time came
she crouched in the creekbed
& bit her lips
bearing down like an animal
she saw the little face
like Nim's between her legs
puckered to cry

she eased the head
as she'd seen her father do
with the new-born calves
of crazy mothers & tidily
buried the afterbirth
the baby was small & white
a nightjar covered in down
it turned its blind head
towards the little breasts she'd grown
but the milk hadn't come

she made a raft
& put the baby on it
with a kerosene nightlight
for company
& set it off
between the soughing trees
the light bobbed & swam
on the flood water
the baby shone
luminous in the glow
Alice waved to it
till it turned the corner
then she ran away
through the bush
her breasts filling up
with milk were aching
Nim   she called   *Nim*
she was almost free.

7

Nim's dead they told her
lying in a ditch at the bottom of the garden
she went to look at him
his small curled prick & fragile bones
the hawk sat on his head
the owl fluffed her feathers on his navel

Alice crouched on the grave of the 28 parrot
the tabby cat & the bantam hen
& tried to think about Robert Louis Stevenson's
A Child's Garden of Verses
this must be what it's like to be alone
she thought   it isn't so bad
then the falcon flew up to her wrist
& the white owl to her shoulder
Thief!   cried Nim on the winter wind.

From **The Infernal Grove**

To start again she said
to recover the child in the garden
reach out push open the gate
by the Geraldton Wax
where the petals drifting past
from the almond trees
clog up the wire fences
time is only told by Four O'Clocks.

To be alone
with no companionship
except the wind   the bird
the sheep   the stone
And Nim   the voice said

*

Not Nim   she struck the wall
but loneliness complete & rounded
perfect in its circle
to see the shadow of the self
go out at morning
& return at night
to be the friend of every living thing
the spade turns up
earthworm & scorpion
the hornet on the verandah
hangs up her home
the ice-cold frog
leaps pulsing to my palm
the great trees stormy-pelted
ring the farm
to hear to see to run
to be alone
with Nim   the voice said

And then it starts again
the garden's soft with fruit fly
the black snake coils
across the path to spring
the sundial ticks
the blood drips down my thighs
everything takes on mortality.

*

Remember how time ran
when he was with you
the talk fell from your tongues
till no one knew which thought
was his or yours so close you were
your bodies lay entwined like children's
while a bough tapped out
against the glass
the breath of sleep.

But where he's been
the garden's desolate
the tree is withered
grass is dry & burned
& loneliness equates
with deprivation
it turns the heart
towards death.

Don't let him in!

But I would rather
live in hell   she said
& forfeit heaven
to have been with him.

From The Shape-Changers

66

Alice knows what death is
corpses glow in her life
the blue infanta
the grandfather stroked
rattling under his awful eye
sad orang-utan
in her bald fur fabric
she's danced a long fandango
with the boney man
the rails fly under her feet
Hoo   Hoo   she   dangles
old Daddy Potstick
playing chicken

I am lonely to my heart
                    she whinges
lonely to my bones
I have nobody   my body vanishes
my mouth is stopped up
I have stopped calling out to anybody
the hole between my legs is dying
the small tuft of hair above its mouth
                              is dry
I am an alien   I must be
to be left here to die
laid out in Darlinghurst
snared by the Early Kooka
the roadpecker's shadow
hops on the blind
under the lightening heaven
she lies dazzled
does everything vanish
every   thing?

67

So now she has given away everything.
          stripped the house.
the money in the cream jug   the silver teapot
the marble surrounds
on the fireplace
the pipes have burst
the derros sleep
in the flower garden

all that winter they were pulling down cars
              & sharpening knives
she took to her bed listening for his step
              on the stairs
the cointreau winked on the window-sill
the old man next door still fed his pigeons
from the balcony   the rain washed in
black & white dolphins danced in a golden sea
he was standing in the doorway holding a mollymook
         with a wingspan of 12 feet

Go to sleep Alice you little fool
      you won't feel the drowning

My exuberant chaotic & wretched life is over
if you sit beside me I won't be afraid
       she said
through rocks & shoals into the bright beyond
shall we have a fair wind after it?

Under St Peter's bell the doberman howls
the old man comes in   *she died in her sleep*
with her hands folded there was nobody with her
don't nurse a grievance   teach it to walk.

69

You'll never dig it deep enough
                    says Alice
standing in the bluish light
that fills the window frame
the wizard's volume under her bare arm.
the church can't hold me
like a maggoty apple
I'll burrow back to him
& she who parts us
shall bring a brand from heaven
& fire us hence like foxes.

Put a rose leaf in your prayer books
                    for me tonight
it's heavy weather
the earth shivers & spins
the shadows float like leaves
there's a subtle chill in the air
& the mass bells ringing
who'll toll the bell
& who'll begin? I says the bull
because I can pull
I'll toll the bell

where are the lips now Alice
that opened to the man you loved
& the strong thighs
that held him close as birth?
Three feet is enough in the clay
three feet of earth is deep
they sleep sound they settle down
the sweet flesh falls off
like a snake's skin

The death nurses are such tattle tails
                    says Alice
five fires & five women
he's had his quota
it's blowing up for rain
strew ash in your hair
& save your skin.

71

She came to the place of the hills
the place of the stone
the place of the sword
the chapel on the green

between a great lake & a sullen sky
the island swam like glass
the winter was quiet
but the coast was bound with storms
at night the forest roared
the white owl with the cruel beak
watched where she sat
low & brilliant the Great Bear
wheeled to the North
I am the keeper of the shrine now
Alice said   *this is the place*
I have been looking for all my life
& now that my life is over...

Nim crashed out of the forest
the island of glass
sank under his feet
no human presence
marked the unprinted frost

There is a holy woman   they told him
who lives in the chapel on the green
la belle inconnue   &   a white owl
that flies up in men's faces
Alice   Nim whispered   *Alice*

He stood in the porch
with the night inside him
What shall I do now? he cried

the door swung open
he saw the white owl
its great eyes blind & wise
Show yourself to me just once

he begged her
it isn't much to ask
but she didn't waver
he opened the organ
the notes were clogged with leaves
the gauze curtain came down over his face
he stepped back into the clearing
a green dazzle blinded him
or was it tears
he heard the organ playing
Blake's hymn but he didn't turn
the island floated
sunlit above its secret
you died   he accused her
you dared to die
one day   he warned her   *one day...*

Alice flew out of the chapel
& circled the lake   3   times
she saw Nim hunched on the shore
fishing   a trout struggled
silver on the end of his line
you are the Grail
& I am the Sword   he shouted

Your sword   she whispered

it was the most beautiful
& deadly sword in all the world
& it was for me
but it was only a fluke
we found each other
& for such a short time

a white mist rose up
obliterating everything
I see things that are not there
said Alice...

the long & terrible cry of the owl
mourned through the forest
& after it   a man moaning
How are your bones my darling?

Nim flies
over rivers & cities
he flies   he is the falcon
small   neat   & deadly
beautiful   as a stone
hurtles   from the ging
he hurtles earthwards
& rises   he comes
to the heart of the wood
to the chapel on the green
in the thin drizzle
he shakes his head
& his breast feathers
knocks   3   times
with his predator's beak
the silence answers him

with a rush of wings
he flies in
when his eyes
grow used to the gloom
he sees Alice blinking
perched on the altar rail
sees the vision of her
she gleams
the wind of his coming
parts her feathers
her eyes glow
Old snowy owl!   he croaks

the candles burn sideways
the wax drips
under his fierce & dreaming eye
she glistens   she is love
his beak curves to her nape
& nuzzles
he strikes down
her soft heavy feathery body
encloses him
it is as he has remembered
I am the owl   she hoots
half-blind with light
& double visioned
is it over?

No   he croaks
it is the beast fable
it is the myth of ourselves
& only just beginning

Come   shrieks Nim
together they leave the chapel
testing the air   they mount
& are borne away

that was the time
when they made friends with death.

NEW POEMS

From Return to the Peninsula

1

We come in the off season
when the rich mansions
the summer houses are empty
and stray cats with bells
roam through the Paradise gardens

the back beach is deserted
the key-holes in the bathing boxes
stiff with cold
except for one slow learner
drifting along the shoreline
in army surplus
his breast pinned with badges

each night I hear the tide rise
but the mornings are like green glass
as if I lay on the floor of an ocean

only the gold butterfly
hatched out for her first flight
stumbles against the melaluca hedge
dusting the death spots
on the backs of my hands
            with pollen.

5

I am the one
no longer beautiful
behind the melaluka hedge
beside the bay
who sleeps and weeps
and sleeps again
calling to you
across the drift of time

I hide in the silent garden
furred with frost
remote and still
where no one comes
where time itself is lost
and the bay runs
like watered silk
through a skein of hills

no one will burst
through the melaluka hedge
no one will open the door
to the silent house
the dark rooms
of the unconscious wait
in a square of sunlight
circled by the sea

the thorns grow higher
as the birds grow quiet.

8

The garden behind glass
moonlit as day
the rain walks through the grass
intimate as a lover
out on the bay
a stormy petrel calls
from its wild domain
poems dance
like firelight on the walls

eerie as white frost
the fox moans
by the front gate
marauding for birds

I lie in the still house
wired for sound
trembling with words
found lost found again
fox firelight birds
fish gut and oyster-catchers
drunken as lords
flapping home through the rain

daybreak   the receiver
clicks into silence
the fire dies
to a smoulder of sticks
the hedge hung with diamonds
shearwaters out of reach
falling down the sky.

Dorothy Hewett was born in 1923 in Perth, Western Australia, the daughter of a wheat farmer. She grew up on an isolated farm, and spent her early years writing poetry, roaming the land and battling with her mother. She was educated by correspondence, at Perth College and at the University of Western Australia.

In 1945 Dorothy Hewett joined the Communist Party of Australia, but resigned in 1968, after the invasion of Czechoslovakia. At 22, she won a national poetry prize. In 1949 she left her first husband and moved to Sydney with her lover, a boilermaker. They lived together for nine years and had three sons. Life in the working-class suburbs – where 'the air is breathless with soot and smog, and the knock-off whistles from the brewery, the print factory and the glassworks punctuate the day' – formed the background to her only novel *Bobbin Up* (1959; Virago Modern Classics, 1985), which she wrote for a writing competition, based on her experiences of working in a large Sydney spinning mill.

In 1960 she married Merv Lilley, a former merchant seaman, by whom she had two daughters. They and her older sons then settled in Perth, where she was a tutor in English at the University of Western Australia. Her first play, *This Old Man Comes Rolling Home*, about family life in Sydney's Redfern, was first performed at the New Fortune Theatre, Perth, in 1966. She has since written 17 other plays, 12 of them published, the best-known of which are *The Chapel Perilous* (1971), *Golden Oldies* (1976), *The Man from Mukinupin* (1979) and *Golden Valley* (1982).

In 1974 she received a three-year grant from the Literature Board of the Australia Council, and returned to Sydney with her husband and family. She has been writer-in-residence at six Australian universities, and has been awarded eight fellowships by the Literature Board of the Australia Council. Her other residencies have included one in 1987 at Rollins College, Winterpark, Florida, USA. She now has a lifetime Emeritus Fellowship from the Literature Board of the Australia Council, and was awarded the Order of Australia for Services to Literature.

Dorothy Hewett has been called 'Australia's most daring and controversial playwright' and 'one of Australia's most acclaimed and important poets'. Her autobiography *Wild Card* (1990) is published by Virago. Her Bloodaxe Selected Poems *Alice in Wormland* (1990) is drawn from her four collections *Windmill Country* (1968), *Rapunzel in Suburbia* (1975), *Greenhouse* (1979) and *Alice in Wormland* (1987).